TEACHER MATERIALS

for Documenting
Young Children's Work:
Using *Windows on Learning*

Judy Harris Helm
Sallee Beneke
Kathy Steinheimer

TEACHERS COLLEGE PRESS

Teachers College, Columbia University
New York and London

Published by Teachers College Press, 1234 Amsterdam Avenue, New York, NY 10027

ISBN 0-8077-3711-9

Printed on acid-free paper

Manufactured in the United States of America

05 04 03 02 01 00 99 98   8 7 6 5 4 3 2 1

Contents

Introduction

Teacher Materials is designed to help teachers begin documenting. This booklet is a supplement to *Windows on Learning: Documenting Young Children's Work*. In the book, three windows provide a framework for thinking about documentation: a Window on a Child's Development, a Window on a Learning Experience, and a Window for Teacher Self-Reflection. As we worked with teachers who were learning to document, many lists, shortcuts, handouts, and forms were developed to help teachers implement the ideas described in the book within their own classroom and school. In *Teacher Materials* we share these forms to speed the process of learning to document, to reduce teacher preparation time, and to enable teachers to collect and display professional documentation the very first time they incorporate the exciting process of documentation into their own classrooms and teaching. Most teachers will develop their own forms and layouts as they become more comfortable with documentation.

This resource booklet is organized into five parts.

Part I. Preparation provides information that teachers will need to get ready to document. It includes material and supply lists, forms for thinking about curriculum and documentation, and forms for setting up a simplified portfolio system for those who have no system in place. Part I coordinates with *Windows on Learning: Documenting Young Children's Work* Chapters 3 through 8.

Part II. Documentation provides resources to guide the collection process. Included are ideas for organizing materials and supplies, guidelines for photos and pages for capturing documentation for all three windows. Part II coordinates with Chapter 9.

Part III. Analysis assists teachers to focus reflection and discussion with colleagues. Forms are provided to guide the process of analyzing documentation. A flow chart guides the process of thinking about the windows and the audience for the documentation. Part III coordinates with Chapters 10 and 11.

Part IV. Presentation provides many forms, samples, and guidelines for displaying documentation in a variety of ways, including a project history book. Guidelines and illustrations are provided for high quality displays. This section shows how to set up displays similar to those described in Chapters 2, 10, 11, and Part III: "Our Mail Project" Memory Book.

Part V. Using *Windows on Learning* for Preservice, Inservice, and Graduate Courses provides a framework for instructors to plan a course of study on documentation. This part provides guidelines as to how an instructor can coordinate *Windows on Learning: Documenting Young Children's Work* with *Teacher Materials* and the video, *Windows on Learning: A Framework for Making Decisions,* to provide preservice, inservice, and/or graduate coursework on documentation. This section includes suggested course objectives, readings, and possible assignments.

Since this book is a companion to *Windows on Learning: Documenting Young Children's Work,* the reader should refer to that book for understanding how to use the resources. Many of the pages in the booklet include specific page references to where information is located in *Windows on Learning*.

Three types of resources are included on the following pages :

- Think pages to guide teachers through thinking about documentation (processes, procedures, and organization)
- Sample displays to enable teachers to begin by seeing what other teachers have done and provide a framework for first displays
- Forms and handouts to reduce preparation time by providing pages that teachers can reproduce, write on, and use

How to Use the Forms

Forms in this booklet may be photocopied for use in your classroom. Above each form are specific instructions for its use. To make room for these instructions on a page, the actual form that you want to photocopy has been reduced by 25%. To use these reduced forms, you may do any of the following:

1. Use the page at the current size with the instructions on it (writing spaces will just be smaller).
2. Cut out the portion of the page with the form and then copy the form at 125%.
3. Copy the page, fold back the part of the page with the instructions, and copy the form at 125%.
4. Cover the instructions with a piece of paper or correction tape before copying and enlarge the form at 125%.
5. Scan the pages directly into your computer and use a word processing program to type on the form.

Two handouts are included: a handout for parents on documentation and a handout on how to view a project. These are designed to be photocopied at their current size.

Getting Ready for Documentation

You can become a more efficient documenter by organizing your materials, supplies, and equipment to match the types of documentation you will collect and store. Use the lists below to develop a plan for selecting and organizing materials for documentation. Keep in mind that if your organizational plan fits your own unique "organizational style," you will be more likely to follow through with it. See Chapter 9 of *Windows on Learning: Documenting Young Children's Work* for an in-depth look at organization and presentation.

> What types of portfolios will I develop? What will they keep a record of?
>
> ☐ Individual child
> ☐ Adult-selected work
> ☐ Group learning experiences
> ☐ Domains of learning
> ☐ Child-selected work

Recording Observations

What tools or combination of tools will I use to capture and share my observations of children? Will I be able to photocopy samples of the children's work?

☐ Post-it notes
☐ Index cards
☐ Self-adhesive file or address labels
☐ Pen on a rope
☐ Apron with pockets

☐ Clip board
☐ 35 mm camera
☐ 35 mm film for photos
☐ 35 mm film for slides
☐ Slide projector
☐ Polaroid camera

☐ Polaroid film
☐ Video camera
☐ Blank video tape
☐ Cassette audio recorder
☐ Blank cassette tapes
☐ Tracing paper
☐ Photocopy machine & paper

Developing a Portfolio

Where will I keep my observations? Will I include them in the same folder with samples of the child's work?

☐ 8½″ × 11″ folders
☐ 8½″ × 14″ folders
☐ 8½″ × 11″ expandable file
☐ 8½″ × 14″ expandable file
☐ File cabinet

☐ File crate
☐ Hanging files
☐ Index card box
☐ Pocket chart
☐ Slide album

☐ Photo album
☐ Photo file box
☐ Video storage box

How will I store smaller samples of the child's work?

☐ Loose-leaf notebook
☐ Transparent notebook pockets
☐ Large expandable files

☐ By scanning them to computer disk
☐ By recording them with photographs or slides

☐ By layering them in a box between sheets of tissue paper

How will I store large samples of the child's work?

☐ 28″ × 22″ folders
☐ Hanging storage
☐ Horizontal storage shelves
☐ Vertical storage shelves

☐ By recording them with photographs or slides
☐ By scanning them to computer disk
☐ By reducing them on color copier

Tips on Obtaining Inexpensive Documentation Materials and Supplies

- Place needed supplies, such as film, on official lists of supplies the children are required to bring with them at the beginning of the school year
- Solicit businesses for donations of materials, such as notebooks and folders
- Buy supplies in quantity and split order with colleagues

- Ask families of children to take turns picking up and paying for photographs at the developer
- Shop for office equipment and supplies at "going out of business" sales
- Locate office supply stores and developers that give a discount to teachers

Considerations in Creating a Wall, Bulletin Board, or Tri-fold Display

- How much space will I have to use?
- Will I need to provide a new background?
- Will I create and border my text on computer, or will I mat my handwritten or typed text?
- Will I be able to use enlarged versions of original photos?
- Will I attach bulky or heavy artifacts as part of the display?
- How will I prevent tearing of a child's work if I plan to move and reuse it in another location or display?
- Will I be able to display 3-dimensional items on or near the wall display? How will I support them?
- Will I hang any 3-dimensional constructions?
- Can I use mirrors or lighting to add interest to part of my display?

Select supplies and equipment from the following list to help you create the display you have planned. For more ideas on using materials to create displays, see *Windows on Learning: Documenting Young Children's Work,* Chapter 9.

- ☐ Simple desk-top publishing software
- ☐ Color printer
- ☐ Color scanner
- ☐ Color copier
- ☐ Foam core panels
- ☐ Foam core tri-fold panels
- ☐ Posterboard panels
- ☐ Ruler
- ☐ Double-stick tape
- ☐ Spray adhesive

- ☐ Dry adhesive sheets
- ☐ Glue gun
- ☐ Small clip-on lights
- ☐ Transparent plastic display stand
- ☐ Clear acrylic box frame
- ☐ Corner mirrors to use vertically or horizontally
- ☐ Large fabric pieces (muted tones, various textures)
- ☐ Art knife

- ☐ Matting in colors keyed to the background
- ☐ Self-sealing cutting mat
- ☐ Scissors
- ☐ Paper cutter
- ☐ Straight edge
- ☐ Yardstick
- ☐ Table
- ☐ Transparent plastic pocket-style holders for 3-dimensional items

Tips for Organized Storage of Displays

- Use a box such as poster board comes in to organize and store display panels.
- Use a large cardboard box to store foam core displays. Cut the top part of the sides at a 45 degree angle to make "flipping" through the displays easier. Label each panel on the back as to project, date, and so forth.
- Use cardboard mailing tubes to store large items such as murals

Displaying in Other Places

For many people seeing is believing. When we display documentation of the learning that is taking place in our classrooms, we demonstrate our accountability and open the door for dialogue about best teaching practices with those in our community.

Which of these locations could you use to share your display? What others can you think of?

Local
- ☐ Staff meetings
- ☐ Staff meetings at other schools or centers in the community
- ☐ School or center board meetings
- ☐ Meetings of fellow early childhood educators
- ☐ School or center institute days
- ☐ Public library
- ☐ Community center
- ☐ Chamber of commerce
- ☐ High school child development department
- ☐ County home extension meetings
- ☐ Meetings of local women's clubs
- ☐ Meetings of local men's clubs
- ☐ Meetings of local professional clubs with related interests, such as the Arts Council or the Retired Teacher's Association
- ☐ Meetings of local service organizations
- ☐ Bank lobby display areas
- ☐ Newspaper office
- ☐ Mall
- ☐ Children's book store

- ☐ Business related to topic of the display (e.g., a learning experience centered on cars might be set up at a local car dealership)
- ☐ Retirement centers
- ☐ Museum

Extended
- ☐ Local college and junior college display cases
- ☐ Area education agencies
- ☐ Professional meetings at the area level
- ☐ Professional meetings at the state level
- ☐ Professional meetings at the national level
- ☐ World Wide Web
- ☐ Professional journals
- ☐ Popular magazines

Additional Sites
- ☐
- ☐
- ☐
- ☐
- ☐

Developing a Portfolio System

An individual portfolio for each child is a means to organize a child's work and provide the teacher with a Window on the Child's Development. A well planned systematic portfolio system can be one of a teacher's most valuable tools for collecting and assessing children's individual progress. See *Windows on Learning*, Chapter 6. Use the form below (enlarge 125%) to help you plan your own individual portfolio system. Carefully reflect on each question as you answer it and begin your planning.

> "All of the types of documentation used for collecting individual portfolios enable the teacher to better assess the child's learning and to plan additional experiences based on that assessment."
>
> *Windows on Learning,* pp. 70–71

The Vision of the Portfolio System

- How will I use my portfolio system? What is its purpose?

- How will I share the value of my portfolio system with others? How will it enhance my ability to fulfill the curriculum needs of my classroom?

- What areas of learning will my portfolio include?

- How will I assess a child's individual portfolio?

- Who will see a child's individual portfolio?

The Organization of the Portfolio System

- How will I organize each individual portfolio? What will I use to store an individual portfolio's contents? How will the contents be organized?

- How and when will I file individual items in a child's individual portfolio?

- How will I organize all of the portfolios? Where will they be stored? What will I store them in?

- How will I organize the portfolio so that it will be easy to share it with others? Will each individual item have a cover sheet? Will the individual portfolios have a summary sheet that can be used to share with families?

- What will I do with a child's individual portfolio contents at the end of the year?

The Evaluation of the Portfolio System

- How will I evaluate the effectiveness and efficiency of my system?

- How and when will I make changes in my system? For example, will I change an individual item to be collected in midyear if I find that that specific item being collected does not reflect what I wanted to assess?

Deciding What Portfolio Items Will Be Collected

Deciding what to include in an individual portfolio is an important step in the planning process. The items chosen to be collected will be used to assess a child's growth, strengths, and areas of need. In addition, each item will serve as a window on the learning that is occurring in your classroom. Reflect on the vision of your portfolio system and the areas of development that you wish to "study." Carefully consider your curriculum goals. Individual items in each area of development or content area may reflect one or more of these goals. Items may be included that reflect the uniqueness of a individual child. After considering the value of an individual item to be collected, reflect briefly on what it will take to collect that item. Remember that any individual portfolio item may be change if it does not reflect the goals that you have set for it. The form below (enlarge 125%) will help you organize your efforts.

Individual Portfolio Items To Be Collected

Write down the areas of development or content areas for which you wish to collect examples from individual children (i.e., Language, Writing, Reading, Spelling, Math Concepts, Science, Social Studies, The Arts, Physical Development, Social Development). Decide how many specific portfolio items you will collect to represent each area. Write a brief description of each individual item that will be collected.

Area of Development:

Portfolio Item Description:

Area of Development:

Portfolio Item Description:

Area of Development:

Portfolio Item Description:

Area of Development:

Portfolio Item Description:

Area of Development:

Portfolio Item Description:

Area of Development:

Portfolio Item Description:

Area of Development:

Portfolio Item Description:

Keeping Track of Individual Portfolio Items Collected

This form can be used to record the individual items that you have collected for each child in your classroom.

How to Use This Form (enlarge 125%)

1. Write the beginning and ending date of your collection period in the spaces provided.

2. Write a brief description of each specific portfolio item above each column.
3. Write the name of each child in your classroom in the spaces provided.
4. When you collect an individual portfolio item, write the date or place an *X* in the box corresponding to that child's specific portfolio item.

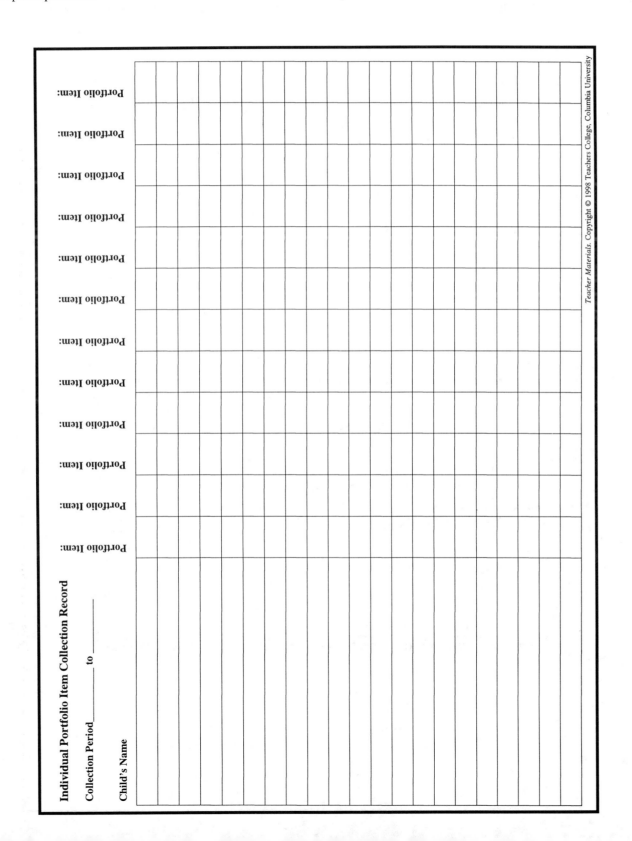

Individual Portfolio Item Collection Record

Collection Period _____ **to** _____

Child's Name

Portfolio Item: (×13)

Sharing Children's Individual Portfolios

Sharing a child's individual portfolio with his family gives his family the opportunity to view the child's development through a common window with the teacher. Individual portfolio items can serve as catalysts for discussions on a variety of topics such as developmentally appropriate practices or a child's strengths. Planning for the sharing of the portfolio allows you the opportunity to make the most out of the parent-teacher relationship. This form (enlarge 125%) will help you organize what information you want to share during a conference. The form can also serve as a cover sheet for a child's individual portfolio.

> "Sharing documentation at parent-teacher conferences [is a way] to be sure that parents have an opportunity to experience the joy of watching their children grow and develop."
>
> *Windows on Learning,* pp. 121–122

Child's Name_____

Age_____

Collection Period_____ to _____

Strengths of the child evidenced by the documentation in this portfolio

Areas of significant growth

Areas of concern and plan of action to meet these concerns

Child development knowledge to be shared with parent (Use one or more individual portfolio items as a means to share some knowledge of child development with the child's family.)

Plans for the future (individual developmental goals, upcoming projects, family involvement plans, etc.)

Documenting Children's Growth in Required Curriculum

se this form to plan how required curriculum objectives can be documented and how you
n show others that children are learning required knowledge, skills, and dispositions.

ow to Use This Form (enlarge 125%)

Copy one page for each content or developmental area in your required curriculum or
checklist.
List the knowledge, skill, or disposition objectives for that area in column one.
Review the web of the five types of documentation in *Windows on Learning,* page 36.
Write specific items or strategies you can use that would most effectively document
achievement or growth for each objective.

> "If the teacher is documenting for
> program evaluation or to demon-
> strate accountability, he will want
> to focus on the knowledge, skills,
> and dispositions that the school
> district or early childhood program
> wants children to develop."
>
> *Windows on Learning,* p. 113

Documentation for Required Curriculum

Based on   ☐ Curriculum Guide   ☐ Developmental Checklist   ☐ Child Development Guidelines

Content or Developmental Area _____

Concepts, skills, or dispositions for this content or developmental area	Individual Portfolio Items	Narratives of Learning Experiences	Observations	Child Self-Reflections	Products (Individual or Group Work)

Planning for Documentation of a Learning Experience

This form will help you think about how a learning experience (project or unit) might develop in your classroom and how you can document each event. Thinking ahead will enable you to organize materials and equipment and effectively use your preparation time so opportunities for documentation are not lost. It is important to plan who will document and how duties of the documenter will be covered to maintain the classroom.

How to Use This Form (enlarge 125%)

1. List the main events you anticipate in your project.
2. Review the Types of Documentation Web in *Windows on Learning*, page 36, and decide how you document each event.
3. Figure out what equipment or materials you will need.
4. Plan who will do the documenting.
5. Consider how to cover the documenter's other regular duties.

Anticipated Main Events of the Learning Experience	Possible Types of Documentation	Equipment or Materials Needed	Collection Task Assigned to	Coverage of Documenter's Other Responsibilities

Keeping a Record of Documentation

Use this form (enlarge 125%) to note the overall involvement of children in aspects of the learning experience (project, unit, theme). Reduce the possibility of cultural bias by asssessing the involvement of individual chidlren in a variety of ways. (For more on documentation and cultural bias, see *Windows on Learning*, pages 147–149.) The form may also help to identify a child who has been especially involved with the learning experience, and use a variety of types of documentation to create a window on that child's development.

To use the form, fill in children's names across the top row, then fill in the date as you collect documentation of individual involvement.

Record of Documentation

Project/Theme/Unit _____   Length of project _____ to _____

Teacher _____   Ages of children _____ to _____

Type of Documentation								
Anecdotal Note								
Photograph								
Checklist Item								
Slide								
Video								
Verbal Language								
Easel Painting								
Table Painting								
Collage								
Sculpture								
Individual Construction								
Group Construction								
Song (Individual)								
Song (Group)								
Movement								
Dramatic Play (Group)								
Dramatic Play (Individual)								
Writing (Individual)								
Writing (Group)								
Storytelling (Group)								
Storytelling (Individual)								
Drawing								
Webbing								

Teacher Journal

Use this journal page regularly to reflect upon the growth and development of the children in your classroom and also your own growth as a teacher. Developing the discipline to reflect regularly takes practice. This form (enlarge 125%) can provide a framework for getting started. Later, open-ended pages or a spiral notebook may be sufficient to start your thinking. See *Windows on Learning,* pages 119, 127–128.

"If reflection is delayed until after a display is assembled or a culminating event occurs, then the experience cannot be altered to achieve maximum growth and development."

Windows on Learning, p. 128

Current Unit, Theme, or Project _____

Today's Date _____   *Areas for Focus of Thought* _____

- Emerging knowledge, skills, and dispositions of the individual children in the class

- Emerging knowledge, skills, and dispositons of the group as a whole

- Strengths and weaknesses in providing experiences for individual children.

- What went well? What didn't?

- Strengths and weaknesses in providing experiences for the class as a whole

- Ideas or plans which might provoke further growth

- Ideas for documenting further growth

- Thoughts and feelings about teaching

- What further knowledge or training might be helpful to me?

Capturing Children's Concepts

Key to Understanding the Diagrams:

A. The original web documents children's knowledge of the topic at the beginning of a project.

B. The words and phrases added in *italics* indicate the growth in the children's knowledge base after several days.

C. The additions in **boldface** show further growth in knowledge that the children used to create the final web.

A web can reflect the growth of children's knowledge over time, since they can easily add information to the web as their knowledge of a topic grows. For examples and suggestions for using webs to document children's learning, see *Windows on Learning*, page 83.

A. Original Web

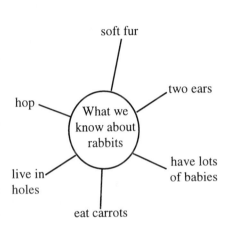

B. Web After Several Days

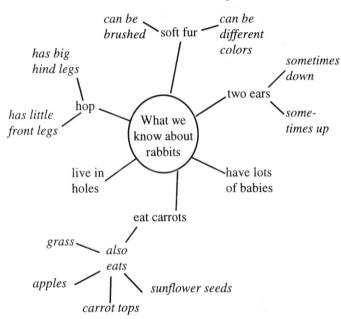

C. Final Web

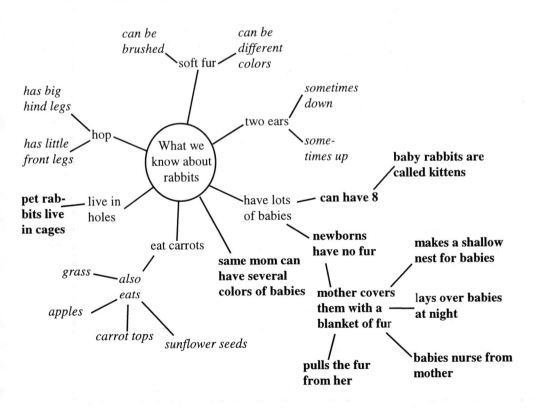

11

Documenting with Webs

A web can reflect the growth of children's knowledge over time, since they can easily add information to the web as their knowledge of a topic grows. Consider the following questions, and then use the blank web form below (enlarge 125%) to help experiment with the implementation of your ideas.

- How can you bring webbing into your daily meetings with small and large groups of children, as well as individuals? Can you make webbing part of the routine, so that the usefulness of the process becomes clear to children?
- Can you provide materials and encouragement for "emergent webbing"?

- How will you differentiate additions to the web from the original web? By color? By dating the additions? By writing style?
- Will you note individual children's names alongside their contributions to the web?
- How will you record the evolution of children's knowledge as the web becomes more elaborate?

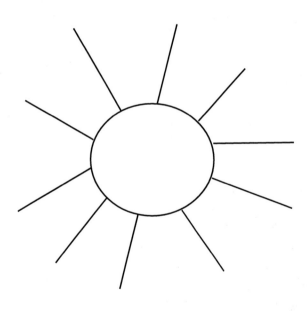

WEB

Place main topic inside center circle, and use spokes to record children's thoughts about the topic.

Date(s):
Purpose of Web:
Creator(s):

Note(s):

Window on a Child's Development

What insights do you have regarding a particular child's growth and development? What emerging knowledge, skills, and dispositions have you observed? Can you describe his growth in any of these three areas as a result of his involvement with the learning experience? For examples and guidance, see *Windows on Learning*, pages 26–28.

Use the form below (enlarge 125%) to share your thoughts on the growth of a child. Be sure to check the box that indicates whether it is growth in knowledge, skill, or disposition that is documented on the form. The completed form may be used as part of the child's individual portfolio, your documentation display, or a project history book.

Window on an Individual Child

Name:

Age:

Teacher:

Class:

Context of the Observation:

☐ Knowledge   ☐ Skill   ☐ Disposition

> This window "provides a framework for the teacher to document and share with others an individual child's growth and development."
> *Windows on Learning*, p. 25

Window on a Learning Experience

What led up to the experience? Who was involved? How did the experience develop? Can you tell about the experience in story form?

Use the form below (enlarge 125%) to share your thoughts as part of your documentation display or project history book. For examples and guidance, see *Windows on Learning*, pages 28–30.

Window on a Learning Experience

Names:

Ages:

Teacher:

Class:

Context of the experience:

The experience:

"A Window on a Learning Experience provides a framework for the teacher to document and share with others a specific learning experience of the class."
Windows on Learning, p. 25.

Window for Teacher Self-Reflection

Use the form below (enlarge 125%) to share your thoughts as part of your documentation display or project history book. Use it to publicly share your reflections on children's work, or try combining it with other forms, such as the "Children's Conversation" form on page 17 of this book. Frequent viewers of your documentation will quickly realize that the distinctive speech bubble shape contains teacher thoughts, and they will seek them out in an effort to get the most out of the documentation by sharing your perspective. For more information on this window, see *Windows on Learning*, pages 30–32.

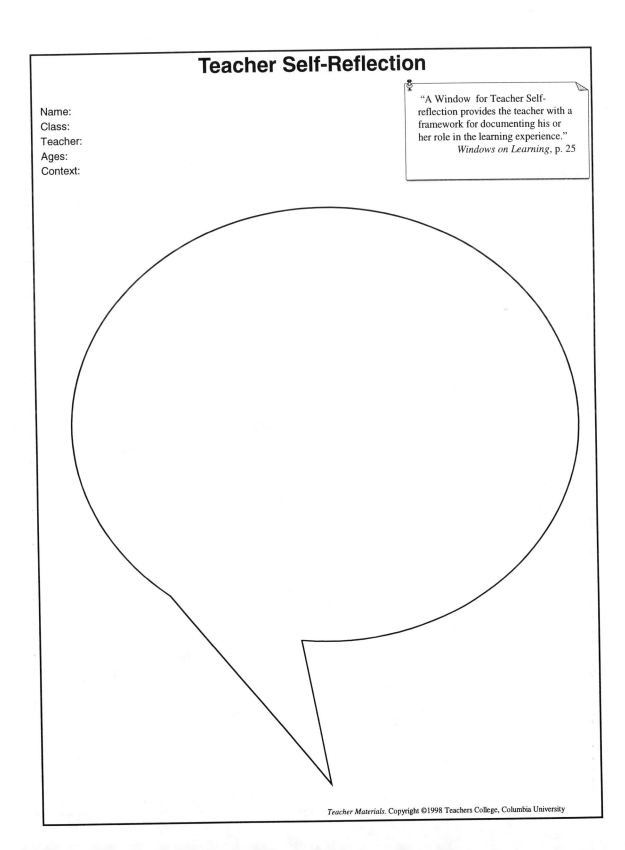

Teacher Self-Reflection

Name:
Class:
Teacher:
Ages:
Context:

"A Window for Teacher Self-reflection provides the teacher with a framework for documenting his or her role in the learning experience."
Windows on Learning, p. 25

Displaying Narratives

Tell about the learning experience, or an aspect of the learning experience, in story form. This will engage the reader and develop understanding of how young children learn, as well as the significance of the experience for individual children and the group as a whole. For examples and guidance, read Chapter 4 of *Windows o Learning*, "Project Narratives: Telling the Story." Use the forr below (enlarge 125%) to share narratives as part of your documen tation display, project history book, or individual child portfolios.

Narrative

> "Narratives which tell the story of a learning experience such as a project can be used to provide documentation for all three windows: the Window on a Child's Development, the Window on a Learning Experience, and a Window for Teacher Self-reflection."
>
> *Windows on Learning,* p. 39

Teacher:

Class:

Names & Ages of Participant(s):

Context:

The Story:

Displaying Conversations

Select a segment of conversation that will help the reader understand the significance of the learning experience taking place. For examples and guidance, see *Windows on Learning,* Chapter 8. Use the form (enlarge 125%) below to share a conversation as part of your documentation display, project history book, or individual child portfolios.

Children's Conversation

> "Discussions and questions are also valuable verbal language products."
> *Windows on Learning*, p. 80

Teacher:

Class:

Names & Ages of Participants:

Context of the Conversation:

The Conversation:

Displaying Products of Children's Learning

Select a sample of the child's work that will help the viewer understand the significance of the learning experience taking place. For examples and guidance, consider the products section of the Documentation Web, *Windows on Learning,* page 36 (Fig. 3.1). Chapter 7, "Individual and Group Products: Seeing Is Believing" will also help you to think about usefulness of products for documentation. Use the form (enlarge 125%) below to share a product of the child's learning as part of your documentation display, project history book, or individual child portfolios.

Product of the Child's Learning

Teacher:
Names & Ages of Participant(s):
Context of the Creation:
Significance of the Product:

> "In looking at the products of children's learning, it is important that we examine and document not only the end product, but the problem solving and learning which took place in the process of production."
> *Windows on Learning*, p. 99.

Displaying Child Self-Reflections

Use the form (enlarge 125%) below to record a child's verbal self-reflections. Choose samples that will help the viewer understand the significance of the learning experience for the individual child. For examples and guidance, consider Chapter 8 of *Windows on Learning*, "Self-reflections of Children: Thinking About Thinking." Share child self-reflections as part of your documentation display, project history book, or individual child portfolios.

Child Self-Reflection

Teacher:

Class:

Names & Ages of Participant(s):

Context:

Self-reflection:

> "Child self-reflections are statements children make which reflect their own knowledge or feelings. These statements can provide a record of the child's emotional and/or intellectual involvement within a project."
> *Windows on Learning*, p. 100

Documenting the Work of Individual Children During Large- and Small-Group Experiences

Documenting the work of individual children during group experiences can be difficult. This form can help you collect anecdotal information on individual children while you facilitate a group activity.

1. Make multiple copies of this form **after** you have listed the children in your class in the spaces provided.
2. Use this form to take notes on individual children's actions, verbal statements, ability to complete a certain task, interactions with the group, and so forth.

How to Use This Form (enlarge 125%)

Child's Name	Individual Notes

Description of Group Activity (optional):   Date:

Objective To Be Observed (optional):

Photographing for Documentation

Helpful Hints for Organizing

- Purchase a camera which displays a time and date caption on each photograph.

- Purchase a date stamp and date the back of each photo or the edge of each slide.

- Look for a developer who offers a special price for duplicates. Keep one set of photos and negatives together in a master album and use duplicates in portfolios and displays. Think of the master album as your archives. Order reprints when you need more copies of a picture or use color photocopies.

- Number the back of each photo to match the number on its corresponding negative.

- Assign a unique combination of numbers, letters, or symbols to each slide or photo when you get them. For example one set might be CP1-1 through CP1-24. This could mean **C**ar **P**roject, roll **1**, photos **1– 24**.

- Start a notebook in which you keep a list of photo numbers and the significant content of the photos.

- Use a fine point pen to help make use of limited space on slide frames and forms.

- Create an album of your slides by purchasing a slide album and loose-leaf vinyl slide holders.

- Don't put off recording information about photos and slides. The longer you wait the more details you forget.

Tips for Effective Photographs

- Hold the camera steady when taking the photograph. Press the buttons gently and slowly.

- Focus on one child or a small group of children, rather than a large group shot from a distance.

- Feature children's work. Arrange the photo so the work has a prominent place in the photograph.

- Show children in action, either creating, studying, or sharing their work with others.

- Stand close enough to the subjects to capture expression.

- Pay attention to the background so that it does not overwhelm or distract.

- Take close-ups of sculptures or structures to show the details of construction. Check the camera manual to learn the closest distance at which the camera will take sharp pictures. The closest distance at which you can get a sharp picture for most point-and-shoot cameras is 4 feet from the subject.

- Take photographs in a series to show the progress of constructions or development of skills.

- Position the camera level with the body or head of very small children .

- When taking photographs that do not show children's whole bodies, arrange the picture so the edge of the photo is not at the joints but above the elbow or mid-thigh.

- In outdoor shots, aim the camera away from the sun so children's faces are not in darkness.

- When using flash, stay within the "flash range." This is the range of the distance that the flash will illuminate. Typical flash range is 4 to 12 feet. Check your manual.

Rule of Thirds

When photographing for documentation, compose pictures to emphasize children and their work. This diagram shows how the application of the rule of thirds draws attention to the child's face and to the construction that he is making. Refer to *Windows on Learning,* page 118 to learn how this rule is applied.

Digital Cameras

Digital cameras record images without film. The images can be viewed on screens, loaded on a computer, printed on a color printer, and used in newsletters and displays. Teachers who have access to the necessary equipment to use this technology may find the immediate access to photographic documentation and the ability to crop, enlarge, and print out very effective in their documenting.

Keeping Track of Photos

Organizing Photos

- Develop a file of photographs that document a learning experience (project, unit, theme).
- Label envelopes with titles of significant events that took place within a learning experience and sort photographs that can be used to document these events into the appropriate envelope.

- Develop envelopes for individual children who have been especially involved in the learning experience. Create a Window on a Child's Development by saving photos of the involvement of a child in the life of the learning experience.
- Collect a set of photos that tells the story of the development of the learning experience.

Examples of creative uses for slides and photos for documentation can be found on pages 117–118 of *Windows on Learning.*

Use the form (enlarge 125%) below to help you keep track of photos.

Photo Tracking Form				
Project/unit/theme	Date	Negative ID#	Photo ID#	Description/Significance of Photo

Analyzing Documentation

- What new concepts, skills, or dispositions are demonstrated in the documentation you have collected?
- Why have you collected it?
- Does it document the growth of an individual child or the growth of a group of children?

Use the form below (enlarge 125%) to help you think about the documentation you have collected. A similar form could be created for each child's portfolio or used to create a Window on a Child's Development.

Reflecting on Documentation

Teacher:_____   Context:_____

Class:_____   Learning Experience:_____

Documentation	Group or Individual	Date	Collected By	Knowledge/Skill/Disposition Revealed

Teacher Materials. Copyright © 1998 Teachers College, Columbia University

Recording Verbal Language

Transcriptions of children's verbalizations can provide an effective means of documenting knowledge, skills, and dispositions. Children engaged in a learning experience often talk so quickly or softly, in quick succession to one another, or simultaneously, that it is difficult for the listener to understand what is being said, let alone consider its significance. A transcription allows the viewer to take time to ponder the words of children and provides a sense of interaction patterns.

> "Recorders with a detachable microphone enable the teacher to place the microphone in the children's work area but to start and stop the recorder from a distance."
>
> *Windows on Learning*, p. 112

Tips for Collecting & Transcribing

- Hold on to your receipt until you have tested the ability of a new tape recorder to record well in a noisy classroom setting.

- Keep several small portable tape recorders in various locations around the classroom, so that you can turn one on quickly with minimum disruption.

- Identify the best location for general recording in each area of the classroom. For example, the top of the refrigerator might be the best spot available in the housekeeping area

- Self-adhesive file folder labels can be used to label tapes.

- Keep plenty of blank cassette tapes and extra batteries on hand.

- Listen to tapes during long commutes to select sequences for transcribing.

- Verbal communication from **videotape** can also be transcribed and provide a record of the child's actions as well as words.

Sharing

- Select short sequences that document a knowledge, skill, or disposition of individual children or small groups of children.

- Describe the learning experience and the activities that led up to the verbal interchange.

- Describe the physical actions of children when possible, since it helps the reader to picture the context of the conversation.

- When sharing verbal language as part of a documentation display, use artifacts from the context of the conversation as part of the display.

- Include samples of the work children were engaged in while they were taped.

- Include your own reflections on the significance of the verbalizations.

Two forms for recording and thinking about conversations are shown on the following two pages. In the first form, each speaker is assigned a column. This format helps provide a visual sense of the amount of participation by each child. The teachers at Reggio Emilia used this type of format to share the language from documentary videotape with us at a Summer Institute in 1996. In the second format, the language of the various speakers is recorded in the left column in order of occurrence, while the right column allows for notes on the movements and circumstances of the speakers. Both forms should be enlarged 125% for use.

Recording Verbal Language, Form 1

Teacher	Marla	Marissa	Emma
A big rubber band. Would you like a big rubber band? I'll go see if I can find you a big rubber band. Remember you've got some tape.	Maybe that will work. I'm gonna' cut some more big ones. Now Marissa, now Marissa, you have to use it. How do we open the bottles?	OK Oh let me please try this. There, I got it for ya.	
(Returning with rubber bands) Oh, you're taping it! Maybe that will work.			

Record of Verbal Language

Teacher: _____   **Date:** _____

Class: _____   **Context:** _____

Speaker 1 Name: Age:	Speaker 2 Name: Age:	Speaker 3 Name: Age:	Speaker 4 Name: Age:

Recording Verbal Language, Form 2

Speaker	Notes
T: A big rubber band. Would you like a big rubber band? I'll go see if I can find you a big rubber ban. Remember you've got some tape.	leaves room
Marla: I'm gonna' cut some more big ones. Now Marissa, now Marissa, you have to use it.	sitting next to Marissa at table, cuts pieces of tape from dispenser and hands them to Marissa
Marissa: OK	
Marla: How do we open the bottles?	as if talking to herself
Marissa: Oh let me please try this. There, I got it for ya.	in a very mature tone
T: Oh, you're taping it! Maybe that will work.	returning to the table

Record of Verbal Language

Teacher: _____ **Date:** _____

Class: _____ **Context:** _____

Speaker	Notes

Analyzing Photographs

It is often said that a picture is worth a thousand words. One photograph taken to document an event in your classroom may have a similar worth. Carefully analyzing a single photograph may reveal information about a variety of topics such as your teaching style, students' interactions, and classroom environment. Select a photograph to analyze closely. Be sure that the photograph selected has some accompanying written documentation about the event that you were trying to document. Use the form below (enlarge 125%) to help you analyze your photograph in-depth to discover more than it may initially reveal.

Photo Analysis

What knowledge or skills is being demonstrated by the *main subjects* of the photograph?

Does the expressions on the *main subjects'* faces reveal insight into the children's dispositions and/or feelings? If so, what?

Are there any *children in the background* of the photograph? If so, what learning is being demonstrated by their actions?

What does the photograph tell me about my classroom environment? Be sure to carefully study the background of the photograph including items on shelves, walls, etc.

Does this photograph reveal anything about my teaching style?

Does this photograph reveal anything about how I believe children learn?

Does this photograph document what I expected it to? Does this photograph document more than I expected it to?

Documenting for Accountability

Use this form to help you keep track of the learning that takes place in the course of a learning experience (project, unit, theme). It can also provide powerful evidence of the effectiveness of your teaching when included as part of your documentation display.

How to Use This Form (enlarge 125%)
- In the first column record the experience that took place in your classroom.
- Use the second column to record the general area of the curriculum that was covered in the experience,
- In the third column record specific concepts the children gained from the experience.
- In the last column note the type(s) of documentation available to support your observations.

"It is important that the . . . people who, for whatever reason, come to view children's work have confidence that what they are seeing is indicative of what is happening to children's growth and development; that information is being gathered in a systematic, reliable way; that children are getting equal opportunities to demonstrate their knowledge and skills; and that the interpretations being made are valid."

Windows on Learning, p. 143

Concepts Gained

Teacher:
Class:

Learning Experience	Area(s) of Curriculum Covered	Concepts Gained	Documentation Available

Selecting Documentation

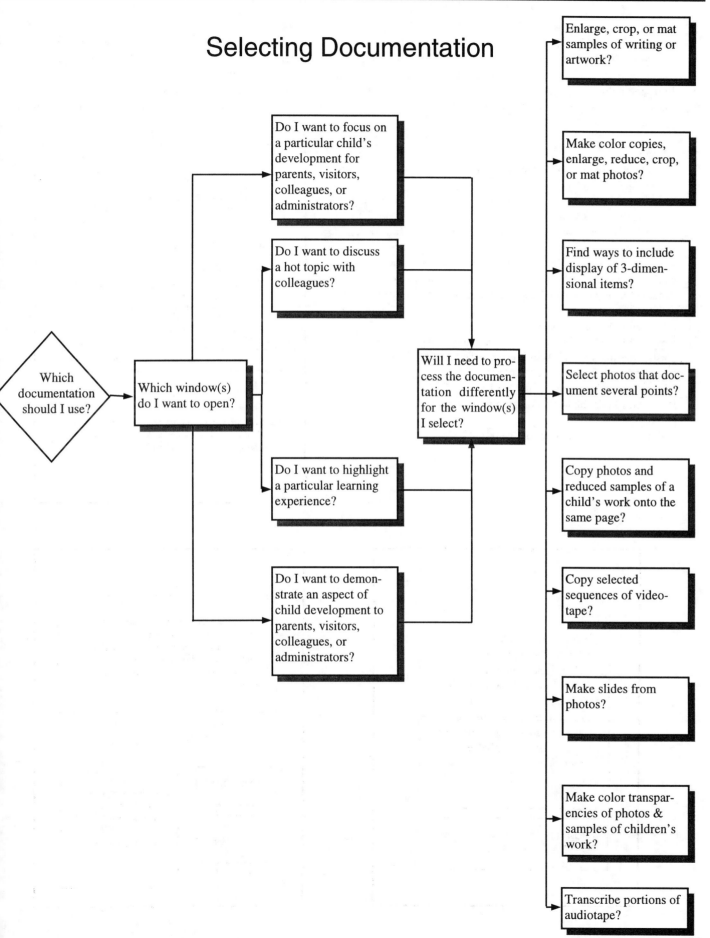

Which documentation should I use?

Which window(s) do I want to open?

Do I want to focus on a particular child's development for parents, visitors, colleagues, or administrators?

Do I want to discuss a hot topic with colleagues?

Do I want to highlight a particular learning experience?

Do I want to demonstrate an aspect of child development to parents, visitors, colleagues, or administrators?

Will I need to process the documentation differently for the window(s) I select?

Enlarge, crop, or mat samples of writing or artwork?

Make color copies, enlarge, reduce, crop, or mat photos?

Find ways to include display of 3-dimensional items?

Select photos that document several points?

Copy photos and reduced samples of a child's work onto the same page?

Copy selected sequences of video-tape?

Make slides from photos?

Make color transparencies of photos & samples of children's work?

Transcribe portions of audiotape?

Making a Project History Book

Photographs and samples of children's work can be used to put the story of a learning experience into book form. The book can be laid out to document the project at both the adult and the child level. It is helpful to include a page at the beginning of the book that explains this dual purpose and that provides direction as to the set-up of the book. The sample pages below are intended to gi[ve] you an idea of a possible layout for such a book. Be creative. Ho[w] could you "open windows" by creating your own combination [of] documentation? "Our Mail Project" Memory Book, Part III of *Wi[n]dows on Learning*, is an example of an actual project history book.

Considerations

- ☐ Will the children help to write the book?
- ☐ Who might read the book?
- ☐ Will any of the documentation that I have stored on my computer prove useful as part of the book? Will I need to reformat it in any way (length, shape, border color, font style, font size?)
- ☐ What kind of paper will I use to back the text, photos, and work samples that will comprise my project history book? What color of paper will complement, but not distract from, the story?
- ☐ How will I protect the pages?
- ☐ How will I bind my book? Will I laminate the pages and use a plastic binding system? Will I use a loose-leaf notebook and transparent pockets to hold my pages?
- ☐ Will I make color copies of the book?
- ☐ How will I keep the book available to both children and adults?
- ☐ Will the book be available for check-out?

Page 1

ABOUT THIS BOOK
This book is for children, and it is also for adults.

- FOR CHILDREN: Read the pages on the right. They tell the story of . . . *(insert the name of book)* . . . which took place in our class

- FOR ADULTS: Also read the pages on the left. They describe the process by which the experience unfolded and include comments on the implications for teaching young children

ABOUT THE CLASSROOM
The Children: *Include the ages of the children, the number of children, the amount of time the children are together.*

The Staff: *Include the adults who have been involved in the learning experience with the children. Remember foster grandparents and student teachers.*

Page 2

Narrative for adults: *Explain what led up to the experiences documented in the book. Explain how the children initially became engaged in the experience and what you saw as the potential issues that might challenge them.*

Sample of the children's conversations as they began the learning experience

---

Narrative for children: *Provide a simple explanation of how they got started on the learning experience. Include photographs and/or reduced samples of their work that illustrate aspects of the beginning of the learning experience.*

photograph

photograph

Reduced copy of sample of children's work (survey, graph, drawing, collage)

Checklist of Possible Items for Project History Book

- ☐ Teacher self-reflections
- ☐ Child self-reflections
- ☐ Samples of children's work, such as drawing, emergent writing, graphs, surveys, maps, paintings, collage
- ☐ Focus on a domain of learning
- ☐ Photographs of individual children at work
- ☐ Photographs of two or more children at work
- ☐ Window on a Child's Development form
- ☐ Window on a Learning Experience form
- ☐ Window for Teacher Self-Reflection form
- ☐ Child conversations
- ☐ Beginning web & final web
- ☐ One dimensional artifacts
- ☐ Narrative for adults
- ☐ Narrative for children

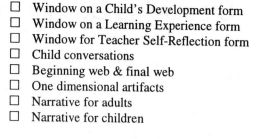

Page 4

Window on a Learning Experience

Explain how the learning experience progressed, who became involved, who led the experience. How did the teacher try to maximize the learning potential in the experience? What issues or problems arose? Discuss the learning that took place and the ways in which it manifested itself.

photograph

photograph

Reduced field sketch by child whose involvement is mentioned in the narrative above

Self-Reflection

How effective were you in this stage of the learning experience? Why? Why not? What principles of good teaching apply here?

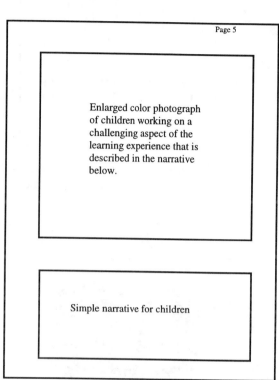

Page 5

Enlarged color photograph of children working on a challenging aspect of the learning experience that is described in the narrative below.

Simple narrative for children

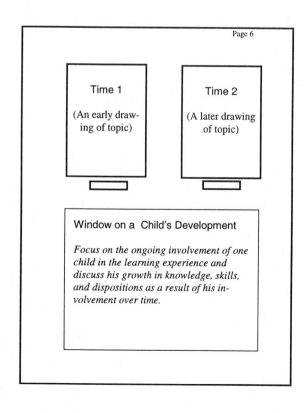

Page 6

Time 1

(An early drawing of topic)

Time 2

(A later drawing of topic)

Window on a Child's Development

Focus on the ongoing involvement of one child in the learning experience and discuss his growth in knowledge, skills, and dispositions as a result of his involvement over time.

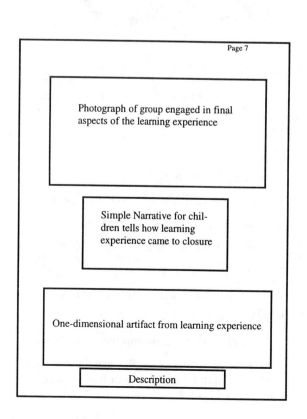

Page 7

Photograph of group engaged in final aspects of the learning experience

Simple Narrative for children tells how learning experience came to closure

One-dimensional artifact from learning experience

Description

Displaying Documentation Most Effectively

Less Effective

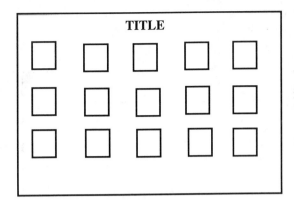

Less Effective: Too many photos are placed on one display, every child's version of the same drawing or product is shown, or children's work has no explanation included.

Less Effective: Bulletin board approach displays teacher's creativity, not children's. Bright colors and commercial art draws attention away from children's accomplishments. No explanation is provided of knowledge, skills or dispositions learned.

More Effective

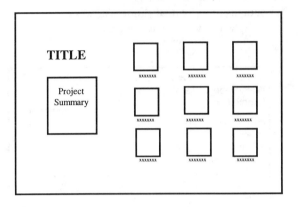

More Effective: Number of objects is reduced. Project summary provides an overview of the learning experience Narrative for each photo explains significance.

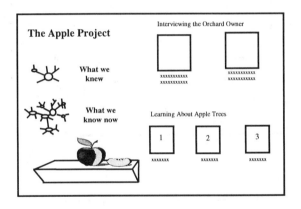

More Effective: Display of documentation shows what childre did and what they learned. Time 1/Time 2 drawings and web show growth in knowledge and skills. Selective work displayed with explanations of significance.

Evaluating Display Quality

- ☐ Summary or narrative keys viewers to significance.
- ☐ Children's work is treated with respect.
- ☐ Curriculum goals and objectives are evident.
- ☐ All words are spelled correctly.
- ☐ Children and adults' names are listed correctly.
- ☐ Most work is at eye level.
- ☐ Colors and background are appropriate for the topic.

Also review the Principles of Display and the ten commandments of museum exhibits in *Windows on Learning,* pages 122–123.

> "When designing a display of documentation, it is important to consider the aesthetic appeal of the exhibit."
>
> *Windows on Learning,* p. 122

Displaying Documentation Using Portable Boards

This table top display on trifold foam core boards shows sequential photos of a project narrative, observation of one child's involvement with the project, and one problem solving sequence.

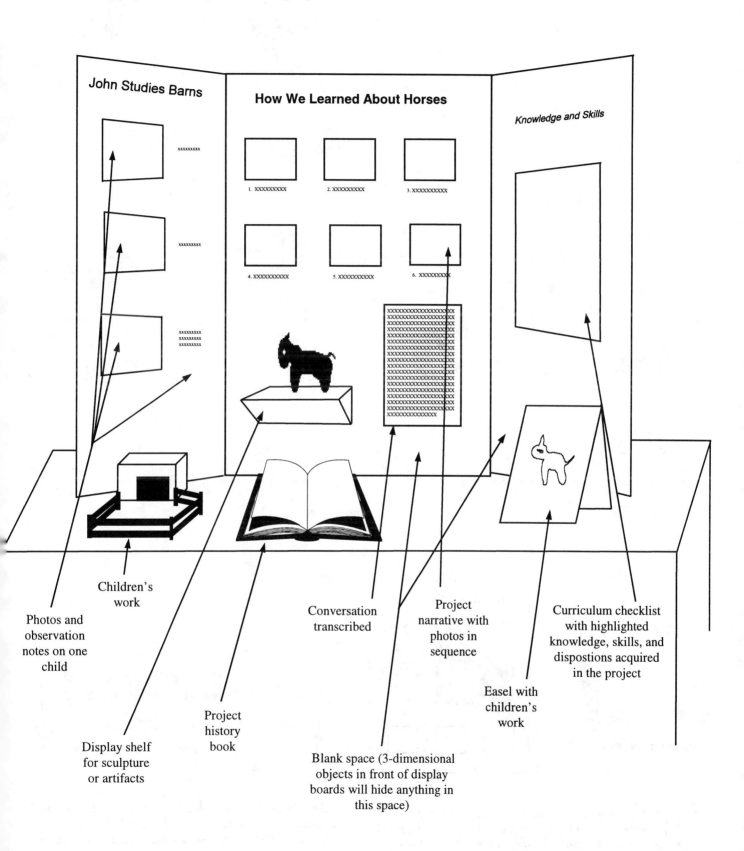

John Studies Barns

How We Learned About Horses

Knowledge and Skills

1. XXXXXXXXXX   2. XXXXXXXXXX   3. XXXXXXXXXXX

4. XXXXXXXXXX   5. XXXXXXXXXX   6. XXXXXXXXX

Children's
work

Photos and
observation
notes on one
child

Conversation
transcribed

Project
narrative with
photos in
sequence

Curriculum checklist
with highlighted
knowledge, skills, and
dispostions acquired
in the project

Easel with
children's
work

Project
history
book

Display shelf
for sculpture
or artifacts

Blank space (3-dimensional
objects in front of display
boards will hide anything in
this space)

Adding a Third Dimension to Displays

Purchase small Plexiglas shelves or make triangular platforms out of foam core board.

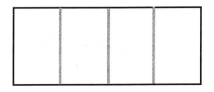

Make a rectangle of foam core board or heavy cardboard. Score and fold into four equal sections.

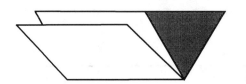

Fold into a triangular tube with the two outer sections overlapping. Glue the overlapping flaps together.

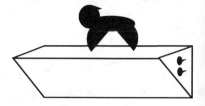

Attach the shelf to the panel by gluing stapling or tacking the back section t the display.

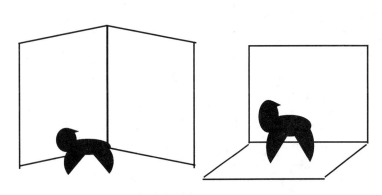

Corner mirrors enable viewers to see three sides of an object. Attach two small mirrors together along one edge with epoxy. Stand the mirror corners behind sculptures vertically or place the mirror corner horizontally to view the bottom of an object.

Collect a variety of pedestals, both manmade and natural, different shapes and textures. See *Windows on Learning,* pag 123–124, for information about how to choose textures a colors of displays appropriate for different topics of study.

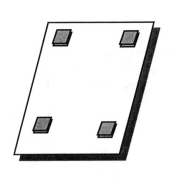

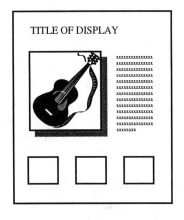

TITLE OF DISPLAY

Add a third dimension to flat items such as photos or drawings by gluing foam core squares on the back of them so they stand out from the display board. Use this to emphasize or highlight children's work.

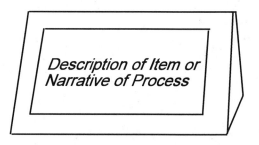

Description of Item or Narrative of Process

Make additional triangular tubes to use as tent cards. Mou narratives or descriptions on them and place near objects c display. See *Windows on Learning,* page 126, to see ho narratives can be reused in a variety of ways.

34

Displaying Documentation on a Wall Without Bulletin or Display Boards

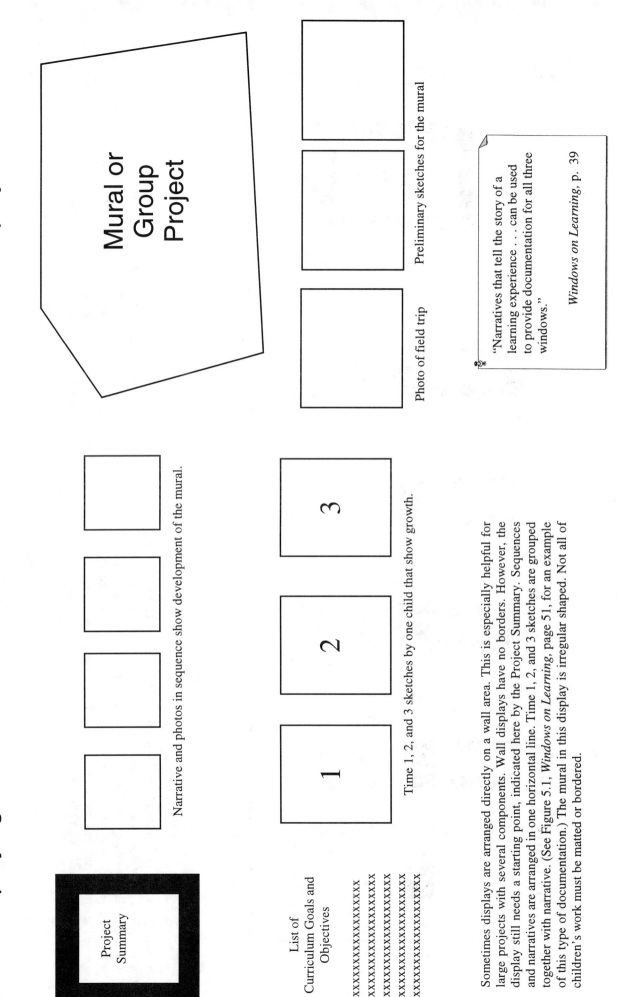

Mural or Group Project

Preliminary sketches for the mural

Photo of field trip

"Narratives that tell the story of a learning experience . . . can be used to provide documentation for all three windows."

Windows on Learning, p. 39

Narrative and photos in sequence show development of the mural.

| 1 | 2 | 3 |

Time 1, 2, and 3 sketches by one child that show growth.

Project Summary

List of
Curriculum Goals and
Objectives

xxxxxxxxxxxxxxxxxx
xxxxxxxxxxxxxxxxxx
xxxxxxxxxxxxxxxxxx
xxxxxxxxxxxxxxxxxx
xxxxxxxxxxxxxxxxxx

Sometimes displays are arranged directly on a wall area. This is especially helpful for large projects with several components. Wall displays have no borders. However, the display still needs a starting point, indicated here by the Project Summary. Sequences and narratives are arranged in one horizontal line. Time 1, 2, and 3 sketches are grouped together with narrative. (See Figure 5.1, *Windows on Learning,* page 51, for an example of this type of documentation.) The mural in this display is irregular shaped. Not all of children's work must be matted or bordered.

Displaying Problem Solving

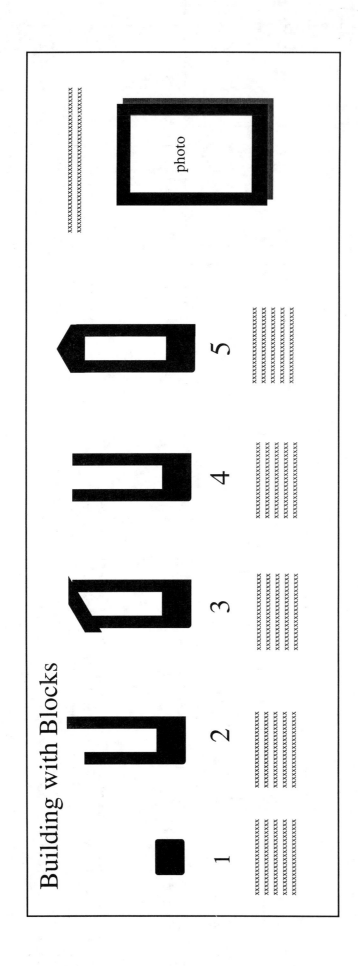

Building with Blocks

1

2

3

4

5

photo

The Story

This display presents a 3-year-old child's problem solving while building a block structure. The display was based on the teacher's sketches that were drawn as she observed the child attempting to create a house with the blocks. The sequence shows how the child selected two different sized blocks for the walls of the house, then discovered that the block selected for the roof of the house was slanted. The child replaced the shorter wall with a block that matched in size and was then able to put the roof on straight.

The Display

The composition of this display emphasizes the passage of time. The horizontal arrangement of the narrative and the drawings of the child's block work requires the viewer to look at each item individually and in sequence. This emphasizes the passage of time. The starting point for viewing the display is clearly indicated by the use of numbers. Each step of the work is explained. A photograph of the final block structure is mounted on foam-core board so it stands out from the background. It ends the display.

Using Technology in Documentation

Videotape Equipment and Materials

Camcorders come in two sizes: big camcorders that use full-size VHS tapes and small camcorders that use smaller-size tapes. Both sizes have helpful features for documentation.

Full-size VHS camcorders record on tapes that can be immediately used in any VCR. They can also be easily sent home with parents. Full-size camcorders provide better picture quality because the tape does not have to be copied, and the video is often steadier because the heftier camcorder does not wiggle around as much when shooting. A greater variety of additional features and accessories—such as sturdy tripods, external microphones, date and title stamps—are available with full-size camcorders. They also often provide more control over basic functions and are sturdy and durable for long-term steady use. However, full-size camcorders are heavy and bulky to carry, and their use requires the full attention of the operator.

Smaller-size, 8mm camcorders and palmcorders require 8mm tapes (which are viewed through a TV hooked up directly to the camcorder) or VHS-C tapes (which require a separate cassette for use in a VCR). Both require that second-generation copies be made for playback through standard VCRs. This makes them less convenient for sending tapes home with parents. They are light and easy to carry and can be used in the low light levels that are often found in classrooms. A camcorder or palmcorder can be slung over a shoulder or dropped in a tote bag to carry on field trips, out to the playground, or around the classroom. The small size enables one-hand use. The operator is not as isolated from the action and can keep an eye on the whole scene while recording. However, the necessity of smaller buttons and fewer features yields lower quality video.

The highest quality videos are recorded on super-quality versions of big or small camcorders (Super VHS or Hi8). Although the quality is better, they are expensive and there are restrictions as to which VCRs can play the tapes.

Remember that parents are excellent sources of advice and expertise about video equipment. Many parents have the ability and interest to assist in documentation with video both within and outside of the classroom.

Matching the Camcorder to the Purpose of Documentation

When documentation will be used for training or extensive study, a full-size camcorder will produce the highest quality of sound and picture. Most often the camcorder is set on a tripod, with an external microphone placed where the conversations are occurring or a shotgun or directional microphone is used. Facial expressions, detailed conversations, and nuances of expression can be captured.

Sometimes videotaping is used to develop a narrative or story, to show the progress of a project, or to enable children to revisit learning experiences. For this type of documentation, a light, easy-to-carry, and easy-to-use small-size camcorder works best.

It enables the operator to stay involved in the activities and can quickly be moved to where the action is occurring. Even the children can learn to use a small video camera, especially if a remote control is available. Planning their own documentation or narrative video adds another dimension to the learning experience for older children.

If a teacher wants to use videotaping for both purposes, a small midsize camcorder with capabilities for manual focus, external microphone, and date stamp, and a strong, sturdy tripod may be the best choice.

Capturing Sound

Built-in microphone

All camcorders have a built-in microphone, and it is important to learn how to use it correctly. Active classrooms where children are engaged in many activities have high noise levels that make it difficult to capture conversations. To learn how well your built-in microphone will pick up conversations in your classroom, record an adult reading to the children. Slowly back away from the reader and shoot video about every three or four steps. View the videotape and note at which point you can no longer hear the reader well enough to distinguish the words. Note the distance of that point from the reader. When you are wanting to capture whole-group conversations or instruction, you should not videotape in your classroom any farther away than that point. Repeat the microphone test at a time when children are engaged in a number of activities throughout the room. Note the farthest distance that you can video and still pick up the audio in this noisier situation.

Sometimes your built-in microphone will require you to be so close to the action that you would intrude or alter the learning experience. There are still ways to get good sound and video.

- Use a tripod and an external microphone placed near the child or group of children being taped and use the zoom feature to bring the visual close.

- Consider investing in a cardioid or shotgun microphone and ear phones for the operator if you will be doing a lot of videotaping and analysis.

- Arrange small-group or individual work in quieter, carpeted, or more secluded areas of the room. Use conference rooms or carpeted hallways for videotaping concentrated sequences or learning experiences

To capture sound when videotaping outside, shield the microphone away from the wind by using a wall or tree. If your camcorder has an automatic level control (ALC), you may be able to adjust it for low-level sound. Check your manual.

Composing Video Shots

Even though the image is constantly changing in a video, it is important to think carefully about the composition of the picture, just as in still photography. This is especially important when videotaping a stationary object or children in the same location.

- Plan what to videotape before starting to tape.

- Be sure that the background behind the children isn't distracting or cluttered.

- When children are in front of a bright light, such as the sun or a window, move the camera so that the light source is to the side and not directly behind the children.

- Apply the rule of thirds (*Windows on Learning,* p. 118) to video composition also.

- Before looking through the camcorder, look at the color of the background and the subject to be sure the subject stands out. Because many viewfinders are black and white, it is often hard to judge this through the eyepiece.

- Use the remote control with the camera on a tripod when the operator needs to be in the action.

- When panning to videotape children moving or running, use a tripod and rotate the camera on the tripod to get a smooth shot.

Create and Maintain Quality Video Documentation

- Buy high-quality, brand-name tapes in bulk to keep the price down. Always store tapes in their sleeves, and never put a bare tape on the carpet.

- Use a heavy-duty tripod that is stable for classroom use. Tape down any cords when children will be walking around the area.

- Always shoot a wall or some other nonimportant subject the first few minutes after inserting a brand new tape.

- Use a remote instead of pushing buttons if shaking the camera is a problem.

Documenting Projects or Other Learning Experiences

- When taping field trips and other group experiences to "revisit" with the video, be sure to capture the whole scene or large features such as buildings. To do this, use panning (slow horizontal movement to show a whole scene) or tilting (slow vertical movement to show a tall object). Hold still for a short time at the beginning and end of a pan or tilt and don't try to rotate more than 90 degrees.

- When recording the progress of a project, have one tape for each project and use the automatic date recorder at the beginning of each day's videotaping.

- Zoom in to show details of children's work or to show faces indicating emotion or involvement with a project; don't zoom too fast or too often.

- Remember the child's point of view. Objects that appear large or frightening to children can be panned for close-up viewing on video later.

- Be alert for interesting sounds to record as well as visuals. (A video of the train station trip is more meaningful when children hear again the sound of the train coming into the station.)

Using Video and Photographic Documentation with Presentation Software

Presentation graphic software such as Microsoft PowerPoint, Corel Presentations, and Freelance Graphics enables a teacher with appropriate equipment but limited technological expertise to share documentation using computer shows, slides, or transparencies. These can be very impressive and effective. The presentation software provides professionally designed templates and step by step help menus. A teacher can scan children's drawings, written work or photos and insert them or use files from a digital camera. Children's words and thoughts can be spotlighted through short sequences of video or audio.

In planning a presentation on documentation of a learning experience, think about the presentation as telling the story of the experience. Begin with a *Title* slide. Use an *Introduction* slide to show how the experience began and why. On the next slide list several *Main Ideas* or events in the project. Follow with each *Main Idea* on a separate slide, with several subsequent slides of documentation to illustrate the idea. Close with a *Conclusions* slide about what was learned from the experience. The *Main Ideas* could be the main events in a project (field trip, expert interview, building a model), main areas of content studied (writing, science, math), or a chronologically told story of something that happened in the classroom.

The presentation software has an outline page where the presentation is typed in an outline format. In writing for a presentation it is important to keep the text concise. Text for slides should not be longer than one line and lines should be limited to 5 or 6. The software then automatically lays out the slides. Each slide can then be viewed and children's work from scanned files, additional narrative, or video or audio files can be inserted. The show can be shared on a computer screen or projector.

If video and audio are not used, the show can be made into 35 mm slides or printed on overhead transparencies using a color printer. The software manuals explain how. Costs can be reduced by using presentation software slides only for text slides and 35mm slides of activities and children's work that have been taken during the course of the project with a regular camera.

An excellent resource for using technology for presentations is *Dynamic Presentations: Strategies for Computer Slide Shows* by Julie Simon Jaehne (Cincinatti: South-Western Educational Publishing, 1998).

Displaying Documentation from Videotapes

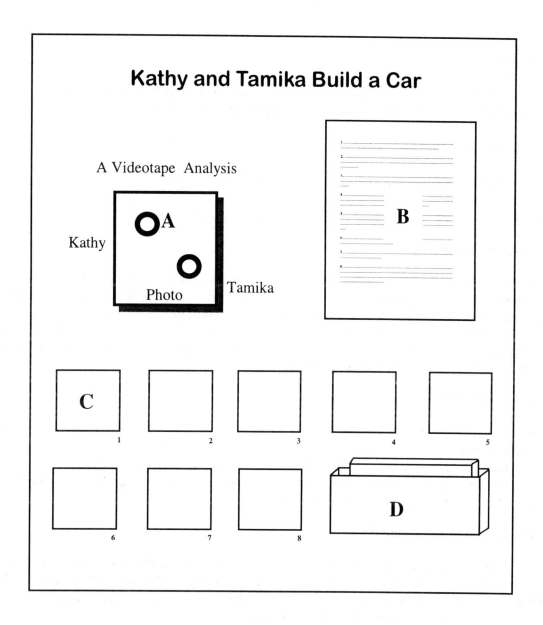

Kathy and Tamika Build a Car

A Videotape Analysis

Kathy

A

Photo   Tamika

B

C   1   2   3   4   5

6   7   8

D

Videotaping can be an extremely effective way to document a learning experience, observe one child, or look closely at how children function together. However, it is often difficult to then share the documentation with a large number of people. This display shows how to solve this problem.

A. A circle indicates the focus of the videotape and the child discussed.

B. A narrative of the videotape is provided with numbers keyed to photos.

C. Frames from the videotape are made into still photographs and displayed in sequence.

D. A pocket contains a copy of the videotape for checkout.

"It is important for the teacher to plan when and how to share documentation with parents. . . . Books about projects, videos, newsletters can be sent home with children. This is especially helpful for parents who may find it difficult to visit the school."

Windows on Learning, pp. 121–122

Handout for Families on Documentation

Dear Family:

This school year, I will be documenting your child's growth and development and the learning experiences that we have in our classroom. Documentation will enable me

- To study individual children and follow their development

- To study the learning experiences that occur in our classroom

- To study my own teaching so that I can continuously improve

What is documentation?

Documentation has many forms: individual portfolios for collecting the work of each child, project history books that you can check out and share with your child at home, wall displays in our hallways and our classroom, collections of comments made while working and in group activities such as circle time, and the work products of the children. Products include webs (a type of diagram) that we make before and after children study a subject, play environments that they create (such as stores), block structures, drawings, paintings, stories, songs, and dances.

Will your child's learning be documented?

All children will have their work documented as we work on our projects. We will document the work that all children do together in large and small groups. Individual portfolios will hold children's individual work. In addition, individual children are sometimes the focus of in-depth study as we strive to learn more about how children learn and develop and may be featured in displays. At some time during the year, your child may also be the focus of in-depth study.

Will you see the documentation?

A major purpose of documentation is to share what is happening in the classroom. Many displays and books are made especially for parents. We hope that you will come and view it with your child. We may ask to keep the children's work for our archives so that we can study it again in the future. In most cases, you will be able to take the documentation home.

Can you be involved in documenting?

There are many opportunities for family members and other volunteers to help document. Family members can transcribe audiotapes into written transcripts, setup displays, make books, photograph or videotape, and take dictation from the children.

I'm looking forward to sharing our documentation with you.

Hosting a Portfolio Night or Project-Sharing Night

Giving families an opportunity to leisurely browse through their own children's portfolios during a portfolio night or sharing the main events of a completed project during a project-sharing night provides opportunities for you to build a stronger partnership with your children's families. Although your evenings of sharing can be very informal, an agenda may be helpful in providing a focus for your sharing. Your agenda should include a time of greeting, explanation of why you are coming together, time for sharing the children's work either formally or informally, closing comments and questions, and, finally, refreshments. You may also find it helpful to provide your families with a short evaluation form at the end of the evening, such as the one shown below (enlarge 125%). The feedback you receive from families may be helpful in planning future events.

Thank you for coming to our evening of sharing! Your interest in the children's work is greatly appreciated. In addition, I am interested in your evaluation of this evening's event. Please take a few moments to fill out this short evaluation of our time together. Your feedback will help me in planning our next event.

What did you learn new this evening?

What did you like best about this evening?

Is there anything you would like to see done differently next time? If so, what?

Is there anything that we discussed tonight that you would like to know more about?

Handout

How To View A Project Display

1. Read the Project Summary

When a project is on display, there will be a project summary near the display. It has a black border and will tell you the age of the children, the focus of the project, and what the children learned. This will provide an overview for understanding the rest of the display.

2. Find a web or list that shows children's knowledge about the topic.

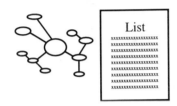

A web is a diagram of children's knowledge about a topic. Webs are usually the children's thoughts and words written down by the teacher. Lines and circles indicate how children's thoughts are related. Teachers do webs when they begin to study a project to find out what children know and to plan the project. There may be several webs displayed: a beginning web, an ending web, or a planning web. Lists are sometimes substituted for webs.

3. Look for any large structure or play environment.

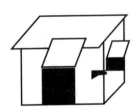

Large structures and play environments are often the results of the children's in-depth study. These are usually large items constructed by several children working together. This process requires problem solving and working as a group. Many skills in building and doing research are developed in the process of making these structures. Children plan the structure with preliminary designs and field sketches. Extensive problem solving occurs as children try to represent their ideas using the media. In the beginning problem solving is largely trial and error. Then they learn to think ahead.

4. Look for children's representation of their learning.

Representing what they are seeing and learning about is very beneficial to children. Representations take the form of drawings, block structures, murals, sketches, songs, and children's writing. Representing helps children organize their knowledge. Children are encouraged to redraw or rewrite as their knowledge increases.

5. Look for teacher documentation of the development of knowledge, skills, and dispositions.

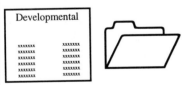

The development of knowledge and skills is monitored through documentation. A developmental checklist, curriculum guide, or list of goals and objectives helps the teacher focus on the knowledge and skills that children are learning at this age level. Evidence of growth in these areas is often provided by marking on the checklist when knowledge and skills are observed and by collecting children's work into portfolios. When developmental checklists are displayed, concepts that were observed during the progress of the project are highlighted. Samples of children's work that will eventually go into their portfolios are also often on display. These items show how children are learning required curriculum.

Part V. USING *Windows on Learning* FOR PRESERVICE, INSERVICE, AND GRADUATE COURSES

The study of documentation can be added to courses on assessment and curriculum or practicum experiences. Coordination of the three resources: *Windows on Learning: Documenting Young Children's Work, Teacher Materials for Documenting Young Children's Work,* and the video *Windows on Learning: A Framework for Making Decisions* can achieve the following objectives. coordinated, comprehensive resources.

Course Objectives	Readings from *Windows on Learning*	Possible Assignments in *Teacher Materials*
1. To understand the importance of authentic assessment and the role of documentation in assessment and teaching.	Introduction Ch. 1: Value of Documentation Ch. 11: Documentation as Assessment	Read: Handout for Families on Documentation, p. 40 View video: *Windows on Learning: A Framework for Making Decisions*
2. To develop a framework for thinking about documentation using three windows: Window on a Child's Development, Window on a Learning Experience, and Window for Teacher Self-Reflection.	Ch. 2: Windows on Learning	Complete the following forms: Window on a Child's Development, p. 13 Window on a Learning Experience, p. 14 Window for Teacher Self-Reflection, p. 15
3. To understand how documentation can assist in applying knowledge about brain development, Vygotsky's zone of proximal development, and developmentally appropriate practices.	Ch. 1: Value of Documentation	
4. To become aware of the various ways teachers can document learning using the Types of Documentation Web (Fig. 3.1).	Ch. 3: Documentation Web	Read and review the variety of documentation types in Keeping a Record of Documentation, p. 9
5. To understand how documentation can help teachers meet increasing demands for accountability and specific curriculum requirements while using active, engaged, meaningful learning strategies.	Ch. 1: Value of Documentation	Choose one curriculum area and complete Documenting Children's Growth in Required Curriculum Areas, p. 7. Read Documenting for Accountability, p. 28
6. To become familiar with the ways that teachers collect, analyze, and share narratives.	Ch. 4: Project Narratives Part III: "Our Mail Project"	Write a simple narrative using the form on Displaying Narratives, p. 16
7. To become familiar with the ways that teachers collect, analyze, and share observations.	Ch. 5: Observation	Observe a group experience. Use the form on Documenting the Work of Individual Children During Large and Small Group Experiences, p. 20
8. To become familiar with the ways that teachers collect, analyze, and share portfolios.	Ch. 6: Portfolios	Read Developing a Portfolio System, p. 3; Deciding What Portfolio Items Will Be Collected, p. 4; Keeping Track of Portfolio Items Collected, p. 5; and Sharing Children's Individual Portfolios, p. 6
9. To become familiar with the ways that teachers collect, analyze, and share children's products.	Ch. 7: Products	Read and review the webs on Capturing Children's Concepts, p. 11. With a group of children, complete a web, p. 12. Read pp. 24–26 to learn how to record verbal language, then collect a sample of a conversation and use the form, Children's Conversation, p. 17 to display it. Select a sample of children's work to display using the form, Displaying Product Products of Children's Learning, p. 18.

Course Objectives	Readings from *Windows on Learning*	Possible Assignments from *Teacher Materials*
10. To become familiar with the way that teachers collect, analyze, and share child self-reflections.	Ch. 8: Child Self-Reflections	Collect a sample of a child's self-reflection either by observing or by interviewing a teacher. Use the form on p. 19 to record.
11. Develop an understanding of how an authentic assessment system (Work Sampling System) is integrated into prekindergarten and primary classrooms.	Appendix: Summary of Work Sampling System Part III. "Our Mail Project"	
12. Learn how to plan for documentation: organize the classroom, select materials, develop a monitoring system, and schedule time for collection.	Ch. 9: Organization and Presentation	Read Planning for Documentation of a Learning Experience, p. 8. Take one activity from a unit or project and plan for documentation. Read Photographing for Documentation, p. 21. Read Using Technology in Documentation, pp. 37–38. Review the flow chart for Selecting Documentation, p. 29.
13. Learn how to collect regularly and consistently		
14. Learn how to share documentation effectively through displays, books, portfolios, and the internet.	Ch. 9: Organization and Presentation	Read pp. 30–31, Making a Project History Book. Make a book on part of a project or unit. Read Displaying Most Documentation Effectively, p. 32; Adding a Third Dimension to Displays, p. 34; Displaying Documentation on a Wall Without Bulletin or Display Boards, p. 35; Displaying Problem Solving, p. 36; Displaying Documentation from Videotapes, p. 39; and the section on displaying in other places in Getting Ready for Documentation, p. 2. Plan and prepare a display.
15. Learn how to analyze what is collected, reflect upon it as a teacher, and discuss implications with colleagues.	Ch. 10: Using Documentation for Decision-making	Complete the form, Teacher Journal, p. 10, to reflect upon a day or experience. With a group of teachers, analyze documentation collected by the group. Complete Analyzing Documentation, p. 23.
16. Become aware of ways that parents can be involved in documentation.	Ch. 9: Organization and Presentation	Review Handout for Parents on Documentation, p. 40; Hosting a Portfolio Night or Project-Sharing Night, p. 41; and the handout, How to View a Project, p. 42. Plan an activity for parents where documentation can be shared.